...IF YOU LIVED AT THE TIME OF THE
American Revolution

by Kay Moore
Illustrated by Daniel O'Leary

SCHOLASTIC INC.
New York Toronto London Auckland Sydney

Picture credits:
The Bettmann Archives: pages 64 (left), 69; Corbis-Bettmann: 64 (right), 68 (left), 71
(left); Culver Pictures: pages 70, 71 (right), 74; International Portrait Gallery/Gale
Research Co.: page 67; Museum of Fine Arts, Boston: pages 65, 66 (center), 68 (right);
North Wind Pictures: page 66 (left and right)

ISBN 0-590-67444-7

12 11 10 9 8 7   9/9 0 1 2/0

Printed in the U.S.A.
First Scholastic printing, October 1997

Book design by Laurie Williams

For
Bryan G. Moore, who demonstrated emerging literacy for me
and
Dale E. Norton, who expanded my awareness of literacy for adults

Thanks to Carol Berkin, Professor of History at Baruch College and
The Graduate Center, City Univerisity of New York for her
thoughtful review of this book.

CONTENTS

Introduction

Have you ever wondered why the Fourth of July is a holiday? Before that date in 1776, the thirteen American colonies were part of an empire of more than thirty-two lands ruled by the King of England. The Declaration of Independence, which was signed by members of the Continental Congress on July 4, 1776, showed that the colonies wanted to be free. But it took a war for this to actually happen.

This war is called the "American Revolution." Some call it the "War of Independence" or the "Revolutionary War." It is usually viewed as a struggle between the American colonies and King George III of England, who ruled the British Empire. But it was also a "civil" war, a war that is fought between people of the same country.

There were people from many different backgrounds living in the British American colonies. Not all of them thought it was a good idea to break away from England. If you and your family remained loyal to the king, you were called Loyalists. If you and your family wanted to be free from British rule, you were called Patriots.

What was life like before the Revolution?

All thirteen American colonies ruled by England were along the Atlantic Ocean. About two and a half million people lived in the colonies.

You could travel on the Boston Post Road from Boston to New York, then on to Philadelphia. These were the three largest cities in the colonies. Other roads went south from Pennsylvania to South Carolina. All the roads were narrow and rough. It was better to travel by water if you could.

Mail went by stagecoach between New York and Philadelphia three times a week in spring and summer, and twice a week between Boston and Philadelphia. In fall and winter, service was less often.

Each colony was interested only in its local problems. The colonies did not work well together.

New Hampshire
Rhode Island
Massachusetts
Connecticut
New York
New Jersey
Pennsylvania
Delaware
Maryland
Virginia
North Carolina
South Carolina
Georgia

The area called New England included the colonies of Massachusetts, New Hampshire, Rhode Island, and Connecticut. Shipbuilding, fishing, hunting for whales, and buying, selling, and shipping goods were important to these colonies.

The Middle Colonies of New York, Pennsylvania, New Jersey, and Delaware had soil that was good for growing many different kinds of fruits and vegetables. So much wheat was grown in Pennsylvania and New York that they were called "the bread basket of the empire."

In the South were the colonies of Maryland, Virginia, North Carolina, South Carolina, and Georgia. Here, tobacco was grown on large farms called plantations. In some areas, farmers grew rice, and indigo plants used to make blue dye.

What did colonial people look like?

How they dressed

Most people made their own clothes at home. Boys wore the same kind of clothes as grown men. Girls dressed like women.

Both boys and girls wore a kind of dress — called a frock — until they were four or five years old.

tricorn hat

mop cap

tucker

gown

breeches

apron

woolen stockings

leather shoes

Well-to-do people got their clothes from England, or had them made by a tailor in the city.

lace cap

tucker

wig

satin breeches

silk stockings

silver buckles

hoopskirt

Farmhouse in the Virginia colony

Light came from homemade candles and from the fireplace.

What were colonial houses like?

A farmhouse might have four small rooms downstairs and two upstairs. The kitchen was sometimes in a separate building.

Colonial houses did not have bathrooms inside. To wash your hands and face, you poured water into a bowl. The toilet was outside in a separate little building called a "necessary house" or a "privy."

A house in the city of Boston, in Massachusetts colony

What started the Revolution?

The first settlers in the colonies liked having British help and protection. British soldiers were there to help them fight Native American enemies and to keep other countries, such as France and Spain, from invading. It was like your mother watching over you. However, as you grow older, you will want more freedom to make your own decisions. That is how many of the colonists felt.

The colonists grew tired of following British rules. England controlled trade and told people where they could settle. They forced the colonists to provide housing and food for the British soldiers sent to protect them.

Since 1760, the colonists had also had to pay taxes for various products. Under a law called the Stamp Act (1765), the colonists had to pay extra money for newspapers, land deeds, card games, dice games, and even for graduation diplomas.

The colonists had no direct way to complain, since no one from the colonies was allowed to be a member of the British Parliament, which made the rules. James Otis, a Boston lawyer, stirred up the colonists when he said they should not pay taxes until they could send a person to speak for the colonies in Parliament. "Taxation without representation is tyranny!" he exclaimed.

After years of protest, the British took away all the taxes except the one on tea. This did not satisfy the Patriots. On December 16, 1773, angry Patriots, dressed as Mohawk Indians, dumped 342 crates of tea into Boston Harbor. They shouted:

"Rally Mohawks! Bring out your axes
And tell King George we'll pay no taxes
On his foreign tea!"

King George decided to punish Boston for the "Boston Tea Party" by closing the port. Nothing would go in or out of the city until the tea was paid for, and the city told the king it was sorry that this had happened.

Some people thought it was time for the colonies as a group to protest British taxes. In September 1774, men from the colonies met together in Carpenters' Hall in Philadelphia. Called the "Continental Congress," this group became the informal government of the colonies.

Bad feelings continued. Finally, British soldiers and Patriots fought at Lexington and Concord, Massachusetts, on April 19, 1775. This was the start of the American Revolution.

Who were the Loyalists?

About one-third of the people living in the colonies wanted to remain as citizens of England. They stayed loyal for different reasons:

1. They believed the king had the right to rule the colonies and that his laws were fair.
2. They were afraid of the British soldiers.
3. They had family in England and didn't want to put them in danger.
4. They felt that a government run by rich Patriots would be worse.

These people were known as "Loyalists," "Royalists," "friends of the government," "the King's friends," or "Tories."

Some Loyalists joined the British army and became regular British soldiers (called "Redcoats" or "Lobsterbacks" by the Patriots because of the color of their uniforms).

Others formed Loyalist units that fought with the British. Among these were the Loyal Greens, King's American Regiment, Queen's Loyal Rangers, and Royal American Regiment.

Many Native Americans, including the Iroquois and Seneca nations, joined the British side. So did thousands of African Americans. They had been slaves, brought over to the colonies from Africa against their will to work on plantations in the South, or born in the colonies as slaves. The British gave them their freedom in return for their help.

Soldiers from Germany, called "Hessians," were paid by the British to come and help their troops.

Loyalist soldiers

Redcoat

Freed Slave

Iroquois brave

Member of the
Royal American
Regiment

Hessian

Many people who had recently come to the colonies from England, Scotland, Ireland, and Germany also remained loyal to the King of England.

There were so many Loyalists in New York City that it became known as the Tory capital of America. Delaware and the southern colonies also had a large number of Loyalists. All types of people were Loyalists, including lawyers, merchants, ministers, government officials, farmers, and workers.

Who were the Patriots?

In the beginning, the Patriots were the people in the colonies who wanted England to remove taxes. But soon the word "liberty" was being heard. The Patriots no longer wanted to be "British Americans" — they just wanted to be "Americans." They supported the Continental Congress as a way to rule themselves. They started thinking of themselves as the "United Colonies."

Patriots were known by many names including "Rebels," "Liberty Boys," "Sons (or Daughters) of Liberty," "Colonials," and "Whigs." About one-third of the people living in the thirteen colonies were Patriots.

When war broke out, the "Continental Army" was formed with men from the colonies and a few men from Canada. Most Native Americans were on the British side, but some tribes helped the Patriots.

The Patriots enlisted slaves to fight for them after England had already taken on thousands of African-American soldiers. Although more blacks joined the

British army, it is thought that about five thousand fought for the Patriots. Since slaves did not have last names, many gave themselves names such as "Liberty" or "Freedom." One unit from Connecticut included men named Sharp Liberty and Cuff Freedom.

In 1778, France joined the Patriots' side. They sent money, troops, and a navy.

Spain and Holland entered the war in 1779, supplying money to the Patriots.

Did everyone in the colonies take sides?

No. Many people tried to stay neutral (not choose a side) during the war. Some changed sides depending on what was happening.

Many families split because of different views about the war. Benjamin Franklin was a well-known Patriot. His son, William, was the Royal Governor of New Jersey and warned the people in that colony not to act against the king. William became the head of the Board of American Loyalists.

George Washington was the leader of the Continental Army. His older half brother, Lawrence, was a Loyalist.

Some people hoped to stay out of the war entirely. The religion of the Quakers and Mennonites did not allow them to fight, although some did take sides.

Others were not free to express openly their true feelings, but were expected to go along with the view of their households. These included slaves and indentured servants — men and women who had to work for someone else for a number of years to pay off a debt.

You could not always be sure how someone felt about the war. There were no lines dividing each side. Your family might be Patriots and your next-door neighbors Loyalists.

In some families, a couple of family members would travel to Britain and the rest would stay in the colonies. In this way, the family was sure to be on the winning side, no matter which side won.

How would your life have changed after the Declaration of Independence?

The Declaration of Independence was written mainly by Thomas Jefferson and adopted by the Continental Congress in 1776. The Declaration listed twenty-seven ways the king had hurt the colonies.

Patriots agreed with the Declaration. They now viewed the colonies as thirteen states making one nation.

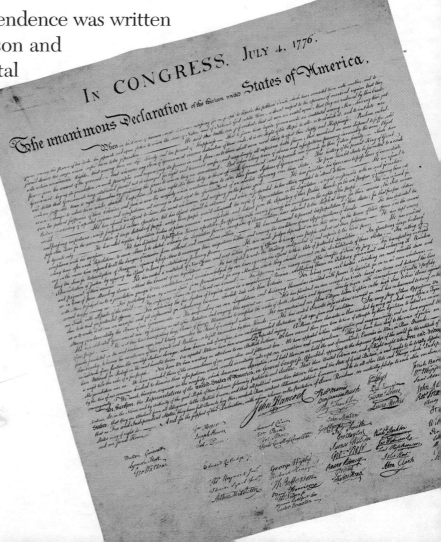

The Declaration divided many families, friends, and neighbors. Some Patriots were against British taxes, but didn't favor a total break with Britain. John Dickinson, a member of Congress from Philadelphia, spoke out strongly, saying, "Declaring our independence at a time like this is like burning down our house before we have another."

Some of these Patriots began siding with the British and even moved to England.

Men who wanted independence went to fight with the Continental Army or with their local militia. In Massachusetts, they were known as "minutemen" because they could get ready to fight in a minute. More soldiers came from Massachusetts and Connecticut than other areas.

With men away from home, family life changed.

Women had to run farms and manage businesses. Children helped harvest crops, and made sure animals were fed and watered. Sometimes, fathers and brothers would return home to help plant or harvest crops and then go back to their units and the fighting.

Money could be scarce for soldiers' families because soldiers often didn't get paid for over a year.

What happened to Loyalist families after the Declaration?

After the Declaration of Independence was adopted, life became difficult for Loyalists. Some left and went to Canada or England. If you stayed, you probably kept quiet. You and your family could show your feelings only if you felt protected by British troops. You might have moved to Georgia, New Jersey, or New York, where there were large numbers of Loyalists.

Loyalists had to pay heavy taxes on their property. They couldn't buy or sell land. In some areas, the land and belongings of Loyalists were taken and the people forced to leave to seek help from other Loyalists. Sometimes, Patriots attacked them or burned their homes.

Loyalists couldn't vote or hold public office. They couldn't be lawyers or teachers. Some Loyalists were put in jail or had to pay money as a promise that they would not help the British troops.

A Declaration of *Dependence* was written late in 1776 and signed by seven hundred Loyalists. This only made the Patriots more angry.

How could you tell who was a Patriot?

Most towns had a "committee of safety" made up of twelve men. Patriots would swear to the committee that they would no longer support or obey King George, or any soldiers or citizens of England.

But just their word wasn't enough. Each man had to bring in two or three other men (called "friends of freedom") to back him up. If the committee believed the promise, the Patriot was given a pass. Men needed passes to travel safely through areas where the Patriots were strong. Women and children needed passes if they were traveling alone.

Patriots who owned businesses advertised that they would not stock British goods. Others refused to shop at stores that sold British items. They stopped drinking tea as a sign of loyalty. They drank coffee or "liberty tea" (brewed from strawberry, raspberry, mint, or other kinds of leaves) instead.

Patriots called themselves "Americans" as well as "Virginians" or "New Englanders." If you saw a man wearing a medal with a picture of a tree on it, you knew he was a member of the Sons of Liberty, a group of Patriots well known throughout the colonies. Many towns had a "Liberty Tree" (it might be a real tree, or just a pole) where Patriots met to talk and plan.

The number 13 was important to the Patriots because there were thirteen colonies. It was often used as a signal. Some women wore their hair in thirteen curls as a sign of support for the Patriots.

After the Declaration of Independence was adopted in 1776, Patriot families celebrated the Fourth of July as a holiday. Towns planned a day of festivities including gun salutes, patriotic speeches, dances, sporting events, bell ringing, bonfires, and illuminations (lighted candles in the windows of the houses).

People sang songs about the leaders of the American and British armies. Two popular songs were "War and Washington," and "General Burgoyne's Surrender," about a British officer who lost a major battle at Saratoga, New York, in 1777.

Sometimes a fireworks display would end with a burst of thirteen rockets.

How could you tell who was a Loyalist?

A Loyalist would not take the patriotic oath.

Loyalists celebrated holidays that showed their support for England. The king's birthday (June 4) was celebrated each year with illuminations, a gun salute, and music and dancing. They sang songs such as "God Save the King," and loudly cheered three "huzzas" for the health of the king.

One way Loyalists identified each other was by asking what was to eat. A Loyalist reply would include the word "tea." Loyalists continued to drink tea throughout the war and buy products made in England if they could get them.

If your family sided with the Patriots, how did you support the war?

You may have shared food with soldiers when they marched by your house. But you didn't eat lamb. Sheep were needed to supply wool for soldiers' uniforms.

Lead was needed to make ammunition, so families donated lead tools and other items to be melted and then molded into bullets. In July of 1776, Patriots in New York City found a good source of bullets — a lead statue of King George on his horse. They pulled down the statue and carted most of it to the village of Litchfield, Connecticut, where it was molded into more than forty thousand bullets for American muskets.

Patriot women stopped buying English products such as tea and cloth. (They would not wear black clothing, even for funerals, because black cloth came from Britain.) They collected money and made clothes for soldiers.

Patriots showed their support by flying the new national flag, adopted by the Continental Congress on June 14, 1777. The flag had thirteen red and white stripes, and thirteen white stars on a blue background. Families displayed the flag on many occasions throughout the year, especially on June 14, which became known as "Flag Day."

If your family sided with the Loyalists, how did you support the war?

Loyalists, even children, became "the eyes and ears" of the British. Because the British were fighting on land they didn't know, Loyalists provided information about roads, bridges, possible spots for campsites, and local supplies of food for the troops and their horses.

Sometimes, Loyalists would make maps and point out possible sites for a fight with the Continental Army. They took messages between British units. Some spied on Patriot troops, then passed on information they learned.

Other Loyalists openly supported the British. They joined the British navy and guided their ships through lakes, rivers, and harbors. Up to thirty thousand Loyalists joined with the British troops throughout the war.

The Loyalists who didn't have guns could help by clearing roads and building bridges. They gave food and other supplies to British troops and helped to hide British prisoners who escaped from American prisons.

You had to be very careful if you helped the British. To the Patriots, this was helping the enemy. Loyalists could be arrested — and even hanged — for treason.

Would you have seen a battle?

The American Revolution had more small fights than big battles. They all happened within two hundred miles of the Atlantic Ocean, and one third took place in New York State.

Some battles took place near farms and towns where people lived, and you might have seen or heard the fighting.

In 1776, Abigail Adams, the wife of patriot John Adams, wrote about a battle near their home in Massachusetts: "I have just returned from Penn's Hill, where I have been sitting to hear the amazing roar of cannon. I could see every shell that was thrown. . . ."

This battle went on night and day for more than two weeks. It was hard to sleep with the thundering of the cannon, and explosions that made the windows rattle and the house shake.

Did any women or children fight in the Continental Army?

Boys often went to war with their fathers or older brothers. At age sixteen, boys could join the army. Younger boys might have played the drum, bugle, or fife for the soldiers.

Nathan Futrell was a drummer boy in the North Carolina Continental Militia when he was seven years old.

At ten, Israel Task left his Massachusetts farm to be a cook and carry messages during battles.

Women and girls took care of the wounded, cooked food, and washed and mended uniforms.

Some women were part of the fighting, too. They carried pitchers of water to cool down the cannons and give the men drinks. These women were called "Molly Pitchers" by the soldiers. When her husband was hurt, Mary Hays stopped carrying water and took over his job loading and firing a cannon. After the war, she was awarded a pension of forty dollars a year for her service.

Families sometimes went with their men and the army. The armies didn't fight in winter so General George Washington's wife, Martha, spent eight years in winter camp with her husband, returning to Mount Vernon, their Virginia home, each spring.

Was it hard to get money during the war?

Because of the war, gold and silver coins were hard to come by. And the war cost a lot of money! To pay for the war, the Continental Congress asked each state to print its own paper money. At first Patriots used the paper dollars in support of their cause.

However, this kind of money lost value because so much was printed and it was easy to copy. Many people called the paper money "shin plasters," because they felt it was only useful as a bandage for a sore leg. People began to say, "It's not worth a Continental" when they meant something was not worth very much.

This kind of situation is called inflation. It got so bad that in March of 1780, a paper dollar was worth just a fourth of a cent! And things kept getting worse. In May of 1781, it took 225 paper dollars to equal one gold dollar. A few weeks later, you needed 900 paper dollars to buy one gold dollar's worth of supplies.

It was said that it took a wagon-load of money to buy a wagon-load of food. Some soldiers even refused to be paid in the paper money at all; they wanted hard gold.

How did people get food and clothes?

You didn't need much money to buy food if you lived in the country. Most homes had a vegetable garden. Also, you could pick wild fruits, berries, and nuts. You could catch fish and hunt for deer and wild turkeys.

Nothing was wasted:

- Animal bones were saved and made into buttons.
- Goose feathers were used to stuff pillows.
- Reeds and twigs were woven into baskets.
- Old pieces of cloth and outgrown clothing were cut into squares and sewn into quilts. During the war years, quilt-makers invented patterns they called "Washington's Puzzle" or "Washington's Plumes."

Patriots who lived in cities often received food, clothing, and other necessities from relatives or friends who lived in the country. You could also trade with Patriot neighbors. Sometimes you just did without.

How did you go shopping in the city?

Loyalists who lived in cities had to buy most of their food and necessities.

It was hard to store food in the city, so people shopped at the market every day but Sunday, when it was closed.

Church bells would ring to announce the opening of the market and the close of the market day. Tuesday and Friday were the big market days. Shoppers went from stall to stall buying meat and vegetables. You could buy bread at the baker's and you could also take your meat and pies there to cook in his oven.

Butter, milk, and eggs could be delivered to your house.

It did become harder to get food in the cities as the war continued. Patriots asked farmers not to take food from their crops into the market to sell. But as long as British goods could get shipped in and the people had the coins to buy them, they had food and other things they needed.

Did you go to school if your family supported the Patriots?

In colonial times in the northern colonies, some boys and girls (ages 6–8) were taught reading and writing in a "dame school." The teacher was a woman who lived in the neighborhood.

Both boys and girls could have gone on to common school for another three to four years, but usually only boys continued. If boys wanted to attend college, they needed Latin school. (Some boys who had to help on the family farm did not go to school at all, and neither did most black children.) Both common school and Latin school were taught by a man called a schoolmaster.

If the schoolmaster in your area did not enlist in the army, the school probably remained open.

There weren't many books to read because books were considered too valuable for children to have.

You may have used the *New England Primer* to learn how to read. The book had a little rhyme for each letter of the alphabet. Before the war, many of the verses praised the kings and queens of England. The rhyme for the letter K was:

King Charles the Good
No man of blood.

That meant that Charles was a peaceful king who did not like wars and bloodshed.

When the war began, a new verse for the letter K was printed. It showed how people felt about royal rulers now:

Queens and Kings
Are Gaudy Things.

Even the picture of King George in the front of the book was replaced by a picture of George Washington or some other Patriot leader.

In the middle and southern colonies before the war, there weren't as many schools as in the North. Families with money may have had a tutor come to their house for the children. Sometimes, a minister would teach children in a one-room school for a fee. Many boys and girls had little chance for formal schooling. This continued during the war.

There were nine colleges in the colonies (eight in the North and one in the South) before the war, but all closed during the fighting. Some college buildings were used as hospitals, housing for soldiers, or horse stables.

Why didn't girls go to school as much as boys?

There was not much work for women outside the home, so many people felt it was not important for girls to learn much reading and writing. Girls did learn from other women in the family how to cook, sew, spin, take care of the house, and raise children.

Some families felt that girls could learn as well as boys and they taught their daughters at home. Sometimes a schoolmaster in a Latin school would teach girls at the schoolhouse during the hours that the boys were not there — between 6:00 and 7:30 A.M. or 4:30 to 6:00 P.M.

Did you go to school if your family supported the Loyalists?

Loyalists felt they had to protect their children after the war started. Boys and girls may have been sent to attend school in Canada, England, or other countries in the British Empire. You lived at the school or with a relative.

If you stayed in America, there were a few private schools, mostly in the South. School could last eight hours a day, Monday through Saturday. On Sunday, there was always some type of religious meeting.

But if a tutor could be found, your parents probably kept you at home and the tutor came to give you lessons. A parent or older brother sometimes taught younger children.

You learned to read or write using textbooks printed in England. Ink was made by buying ink powder and mixing it with water.

You may also have learned to speak French, dance, and play a musical instrument.

Poor children in the South may have gone to "field schools," where lessons were taught outdoors by some adult.

Slaves, even if they supported the British cause, were not usually provided with any education.

How did you get news about the war and what was happening in the other colonies?

Getting news was important to the Patriots even before the war began. Each colony had set up a "committee of correspondence," who hired its own riders to carry messages by horseback. (This was long before the telephone, radio, television, or even the telegraph had been invented.)

Messages were delivered from one town to the next until all colonies received the news.

Sometimes, information was sent by ship instead of overland.

After the war began, the committees of correspondence

formed "committees of safety." Their riders were constantly in danger of being captured by the British.

Children were sometimes used as messengers. One young messenger was nine-year-old John Quincy Adams, who later became the sixth president of the United States. He took messages from his mother, Abigail, in Braintree, Massachusetts, to his father, John, in Boston.

Another way to find out the news was from a newspaper. The *Boston Gazette* and the *South Carolina Gazette* were two papers that reported news with a Patriot view. The *Royal Gazette* (New York) was the best known of the Loyalist newspapers.

Most newspapers were printed only once a week and had four pages, with three columns on each page.

In small towns a "town crier," sometimes a schoolboy, might share news aloud. As more and more people learned to read, there was less need to have a town crier.

Pamphlets and books were also printed. Thomas Paine's *Common Sense* had sent the idea of freedom throughout the colonies when it was published in January of 1776. It was often re-read and shared during the war. On the last page in bold letters were the words, **"THE FREE AND INDEPENDENT STATES OF AMERICA."**

As thousands of people read the forty-seven pages, they saw themselves as the "United States."

More news could be found on posters, called broadsides, that were nailed to trees, poles, and buildings. Broadsides were used to get men to join the army and for various public announcements.

Who were the famous Patriots?

The most well known were the men who helped promote the idea of freedom.

George Washington

George Washington, a planter and soldier from Virginia, was chosen to be commander of the Continental Army. Called "the Father of Our Country," Washington was a strong leader who held the army together when the soldiers faced many problems.

Patrick Henry from Virginia was known as "the Son of Thunder" because of his patriotic speeches. He started many people thinking about freedom when he said, "Give me liberty or give me death."

Patrick Henry

Paul Revere was a silversmith in Boston. He was a leader of the Sons of Liberty, a messenger, and a secret agent for the Patriots. On April 18, 1775, Revere made his famous midnight ride from Boston to Lexington, Massachusetts, to warn the citizens that the British army was on its way. Revere was captured, but he escaped safely. The next day, the battle of Lexington and Concord marked the beginning of the American Revolution.

Paul Revere

John Adams, Benjamin Franklin, and **Thomas Jefferson** were the most well known of the committee who wrote the Declaration of Independence. Jefferson did most of the actual writing.

Thomas Jefferson

Benjamin Franklin

John Adams

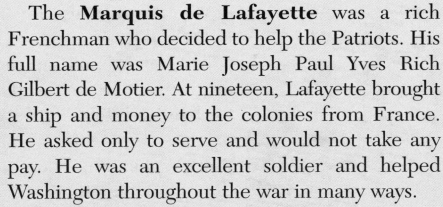

The **Marquis de Lafayette** was a rich Frenchman who decided to help the Patriots. His full name was Marie Joseph Paul Yves Rich Gilbert de Motier. At nineteen, Lafayette brought a ship and money to the colonies from France. He asked only to serve and would not take any pay. He was an excellent soldier and helped Washington throughout the war in many ways.

A schoolmaster who joined the army at the start of the war, **Nathan Hale** volunteered to spy for the Patriots, but was caught by the British. Before he was hung, he is reported to have said, "I only regret I have but one life to lose for my country."

Crispus Attucks was a black man killed during the "Boston Massacre" in 1770, when five people were shot by British soldiers. This event pushed many people to join the Patriots.

Marquis de Lafayette

Abigail Adams

Women were also interested in rights and freedom.

Abigail Adams ran the family farm in Massachusetts while husband John was working in the Continental Congress in Philadelphia. She wrote letters to him, reminding him "not to forget the ladies" as Congress was writing laws for the new government.

Mercy Otis Warren

Mercy Otis Warren was James Otis's sister. An excellent writer, she wrote plays that made fun of the British. Printed in pamphlets, her plays were very popular. Later, she wrote three books that described the events of the American Revolution.

Phillis Wheatley was an African girl brought to the colonies as a slave. Bought by the Wheatley family, she learned to read and write, and wrote poetry. Phillis wrote a poem for General Washington and visited him at army headquarters. She is known as the first published black woman poet in America.

Deborah Sampson dressed in men's clothes and joined the Continental Army in 1782 as Robert Shurtleff. She received an honorable discharge for her work as a soldier when her identity was discovered in 1783.

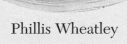

Phillis Wheatley

John Singleton Copley

Who were the famous Loyalists?

Because the Loyalists were on the losing side of the war, their names are not as well known today as those of the Patriots.

John Singleton Copley was a painter who painted portraits of Paul Revere and Samuel Adams before leaving for England. It was his father-in-law's tea that was destroyed during the Boston Tea Party.

Samuel Quincy was a lawyer whose father, brother, and wife were Patriots. It was his duty to try to convict the British soldiers involved in the "Boston Massacre." His brother, Josiah, worked with John Adams to defend the soldiers.

Joseph Galloway

Joseph Galloway was a Pennsylvania delegate to the Continental Congress, but later became the leader of the Loyalists in Philadelphia. He finally joined the British army and left America in 1778.

Dr. Benjamin Church of Boston was thought to be a strong Patriot and was head of the doctors taking care of the wounded Patriots. But he was really a Loyalist spy who was captured when he sent a coded message to a British officer, telling about the size and strength of the Continental Army. He was put into prison for several years, then sent to the West Indies and told not to return.

Thomas Hutchinson was the governor of Massachusetts. The Boston Tea Party happened when he insisted that the tea be unloaded

Flora MacDonald came to North Carolina from Scotland with her husband, Allan. She had been active in politics before she came to the colonies. Now she rode around the countryside getting soldiers to join the Royal American Regiment.

Thomas Hutchinson

What useful things were invented during the war?

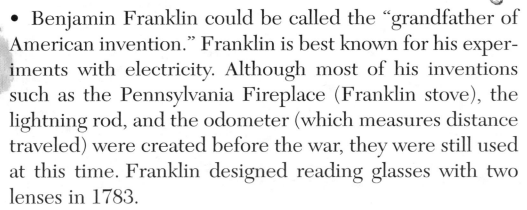

• Benjamin Franklin could be called the "grandfather of American invention." Franklin is best known for his experiments with electricity. Although most of his inventions such as the Pennsylvania Fireplace (Franklin stove), the lightning rod, and the odometer (which measures distance traveled) were created before the war, they were still used at this time. Franklin designed reading glasses with two lenses in 1783.

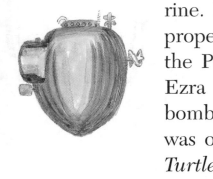

• David Bushnell made the *Turtle*, an early submarine. Looking like a large oak barrel, it moved when a propeller was turned by hand. Bushnell presented it to the Patriots as a way to put bombs on British warships. Ezra Lee made the first try, but he couldn't get the bomb to stick to the ship. Lee had to work fast — there was only enough air for thirty minutes underwater. The *Turtle* never worked like Bushnell hoped, but he built underwater mines that made the British navy very nervous.

• George Washington felt that the most outstanding soldiers should receive some type of award. In 1782, he started giving the "Badge of Military Merit," which later became the Purple Heart. This medal is now given to all soldiers wounded in battle.

What words and expressions came from life during the American Revolution?

• To put your **"John Hancock"** on paper means to sign your name. Why? John Hancock was the first Patriot to sign the Declaration of Independence. He made his signature very large. He said he wanted to be sure the king could see it.

• The word **"cowboy"** was first used to name pro-British outlaws. They used cowbells to attract people and then robbed them or stole animals from farmers and sold them to the British army.

• Pro-Patriot outlaws were called **"skinners"** because they took all of a person's belongings so that they were left with only their bare skin.

- Calling a person a **"big wig"** was an insult. While wigs were worn by many people, to wear a large hairstyle was thought to be showing off or making yourself look important.

- **"The Yankey's Return from Camp"** was a song sung by the British to make fun of the colonists. However, the Patriots liked the song and they turned it into a symbol of the new country. It is still sung today. We call it "Yankee Doodle."

What ended the war?

After over six years of fighting, the British army gave up to the American forces at 2 P.M. on October 19, 1781, at Yorktown, Virginia. General Charles Cornwallis said he was too ill to surrender personally to General Washington. And so British General Charles O'Hara surrendered to American General Benjamin Lincoln at Yorktown. The British officer presented his sword and the American

This old copy of "Yankee Doodle" shows all 14 verses.

tapped it as an acceptance of surrender. The British fifes played the song, "The World Turned Upside Down." This was a good tune because life in America changed greatly after this day.

News of the surrender spread throughout the states by messengers, newspapers, and broadsides. It reached Philadelphia on October 22 and Boston on October 27. Towns celebrated with cannon salutes, bonfires, and fireworks. People kept the lamps in their houses lit all night. Loyalists had to keep their lights on, too.

It took until September 1783 for the final peace agreement to be written. The Treaty of Paris really ended the American Revolution. In the treaty, the new country was recognized and its boundaries decided. Fishing limits were set along the coast of Canada.

It was also agreed that Congress would recommend to the states that they restore property to any Loyalists who had not fought in the war. In most cases, the states did not do this.

How did life change for the Loyalists after the war?

The following verse from a song written after the victory at Yorktown shows that life for the Loyalists was going to get even harder:

> Now Tories all, what can ye say?
> Come — is not this a griper,
> That while your hopes are danced away,
> Tis you must pay the Piper?

After Cornwallis's defeat, many Loyalists quickly moved to England, Canada, the West Indies, or British-held East Florida. They asked the British government to pay them for their lost property. Those who did get paid received less than half of the value of what was lost. Most Loyalists did not get back the type of life they had before the war started.

Slaves who had fought for the British were given their freedom. Some moved to the same countries as the other

Loyalists or to Sierra Leone in Africa. Some joined the British navy. Native Americans, like the Iroquois, who had helped the British, had their villages burned, lost much of their land, and were never able to return to their former ways.

How did life change for the Patriots after the war?

After a lot of celebrating, the Patriots worked to remove the memory of the British. Place names were changed. The Queen's Head Tavern in New York became the Fraunces Tavern again after its owner Samuel Fraunces, who later became the steward of Washington's household. Hutchinson Street in Boston, named for Loyalist Governor Thomas Hutchinson, was renamed Pearl Street.

Some names honored Patriot leaders. Washington College in Maryland was the first college named for George Washington. Mountains, towns, lakes, and counties were also given his name.

Other colleges reopened and college textbooks that had all come from Europe were now printed in America. Noah Webster's *American Spelling Book* (1783) used American spellings and word usage.

Patriotic themes were popular in writings and paintings. In 1793, *A History of the Revolution* was published for children.

The Great Seal of the United States, with the motto "E Pluribus Unum" (a Latin phrase meaning "one out of many"), started appearing on official papers after it was adopted in 1782. Pictures of eagles were also popular because the eagle was chosen as the national bird (although Benjamin Franklin thought the turkey was a better choice). Children were named "Independence," "Peace," "Joy," and "Thanks."

Being a new, free country brought problems, too, especially with money. Soldiers had been promised bonus money to stay in the army but the government didn't have

the cash. The soldiers were told they would be paid in money or land at some time in the future. It took until 1789, when a new central government was formed, for the nation to start redeeming its promise notes.

Products from England flowed into the country but exports dropped. American merchants, shipbuilders, and fishermen could not compete with other countries when England put a tax on American goods going into England.

Congress decided to form a government with a president, not a king. They looked to George Washington again. He became the first President of the United States in 1789 and guided the new nation until 1797.

Author's Note

Information about the life of the Loyalists during the American Revolution is not as easy to find as facts about the Patriots. Because Loyalists supported what Americans view as the losing side, their stories were not considered as important and weren't kept as carefully. Only recently have attempts been made to publish information about Loyalists for older students. They are still not detailed often in textbooks written for young readers.

It is important to understand that war involves people. One side will win in the end, but even in winning, things are lost and people are hurt. America lost many creative people because of the American Revolution. Between sixty thousand to eighty thousand Loyalists left the country. These people made many contributions in their new homes, especially in Canada. Believing differently from the Patriots did not make the Loyalists "bad." I hope that, having read the information in this book, you will remember to look at all points of view before making judgments about winners and losers.

...IF YOU LIVED AT THE TIME OF THE

American Revolution